A Soul Adrift

Miranda Leigh

Wild Dreams Publishing
A publication of Wild Dreams Publishing
Traralgon, Vic
© 2019 by Miranda Leigh
All rights reserved, including the right of reproduction in whole or in part in any form.
Wild Dreams Publishing is a registered trademark of Wild Dreams Publishing.
Manufactured in Australia.
All rights reserved.
Cover © YM Zachery

Dedications

I would like to dedicate this book to my friends and family. I believe in every one of you and I am grateful for every one of you. Thank you for your love, support, advice and friendship.

To my amazing daughter,
You are truly beautiful on the inside and out. Always be who you are.

To Brooke,
my yoga Bestie ♡

Namaste

Mimi

Dive

Dive

Into the waters

Shallow to the deep

Explore what lies beneath

What's left to discover

Buried within your core

Waiting to be uncovered

What will rise up to the surface

Surrender to the shore

Adrift

I feel the waves beating

With the rhythm of my soul

And the breezes inviting me

To drift away

In my eyes you can see

The shadows of the raging tempest

Dying to set me free

Lost

The rich black sky

Surrounds you

Full of priceless gold stars

That fall just beyond your grasp

Your hand reaches out into the night

Wandering through the warm breeze

Your mind wanders as well

You lose yourself in your thoughts

Laughter echoes around you

The trees take on the shapes of people

Their branches reaching out to you

But you remain lost

Words

Thoughtless chatter
Rolling off your tongue
Shallow and empty

Pouring from your soul
Deep and powerful
Cutting through your skin
Breaking down your walls

Escaping your mind
To create and inspire
Evoke emotion
Fill a void

A release and a comfort
A whisper and a song
Everything and nothing

When it's all been said
Surrender to the silence
That speaks volumes

The Flame

The Flame

The spirit

Wanders aimlessly

Lost and searching

Burning one moment,

One day vanished

Swallowed by the winds

Swept into another world

Just another star

Just another shadow

Lost Touch

I lost touch with reality

I lost touch with sanity

I lost touch with my own soul

When I was no longer allowed

To touch yours

Want

I want to feel your rhythm

I want to touch your soul

I want to taste your love

Awaken your smile

Feed your spirit

Release your desire

I want to

Stay like this

Complete and whole

Just for a while

Comfort

Your voice reaches me

With all the comforts

Of loud music

And your touch

There is no word powerful

Enough to express

The depth of which

It completes my soul

Spinning

What happens when

The world stops spinning

Stops you in your tracks

Is life just sucked into the depths

Of a deadly current

A realm of nothingness

Without a chance to escape

Or is the sea of darkness

A welcome salvation

Cold

Your words are

Cold and harsh like winter

They roll off your tongue

And like your cautious step

They break the ice

Your eyes burn into me

Like blazing fire

Tears flow down my cheeks

Rivers flowing endlessly

As your words hit me

With the force of your fist

Your message is sharp and clear

Like glass

It cuts through my heart

Which begins to bleed

Gone

I'm deaf, I'm blind

I can't say where I've been

I'm so far gone

The most piercing scream

Cannot reach me

Not here in my insanity

Where the tears fall endlessly

And my soul

Is empty and bruised

From the pain of this life

Music

I can't seem to get you

Out of my head

You came along when I thought

I was dead

You heard the music

In my laughter

You are exactly what I was after

Once Again

I feel your presence

As you enter my room

The first time I saw you

The last time I saw you

And now standing there

Silence speaks for our

Speechless souls

My memory failed to do you justice

The years unfold

As I melt into you

Once again

Fade

I will not fade
I will not go away
I will not fade from this love
And this love will not fade from me
We will stay
together happily
For one eternity and another

Tide

Facing the tide

High and powerful

Staring into the sun

Setting over the waves of blue

Feeling the white grains

Of sand beneath my bare feet

Smelling the salty breezes

And dreaming of you

Freedom exists

Freedom exists

In its most pure and simple form

Within your soul

Treasured

My most valuable possession

My most treasured gift

Is the love

That blew into my life

When you opened my eyes

With your kiss

Delusion

Locked inside your soul
Trapped within four walls
That seem to mold
into one big cage
You sense fear
Knocking on the door
You say hello
And reality escapes
Sucked into a realm of delusion

Everything

Everything seemed so small
My passion lost its path somehow
And now everything is magnified
But it's not the same
My love for you grew greater
And a simple realization struck
That without it
I am merely a lost soul
In its most feeble state
Weakened and waiting
To be ignited once again
By your flame

With a smile

I saw you in a dream

And I knew you were the one

The way you looked at me

The way I felt in your arms

Everything was perfect

So beautiful

We danced in the warm white sand

The crashing waves

kissed my bare feet

My soul was complete

And I awakened in an empty bed

With a smile

Enough

This is where I go

To get lost in the flow

To move forward

To let go

When I leave the room

I know

I will feel alive

I will find my drive

To move forward

To let go

To survive

With my heart open wide

With my mind ready

With my body free

To just be me

I can finally see

I am enough

Light

I can feel your soul shine

Through the shadows and rainbows

Of everyday life

A light so vivid

Infinite and true

I can feel your soul shine

A warm embrace

That holds me

Through waves of pleasure

Waves of pain

It is my fuel , my fire

My vast desire

The light of your soul

Inspires a love in mine

So bright

So vivid

So infinite and true

It blinds me engulfs me

Carries me through

The tides of time

Is it You?

That dances in the fire

Is it you?

 that breathes under water

Is it you?

that can survive the fall

Lifeless

The divine unknown faces
That light up the vast heavens
Creation of beauty
That fuels the earth
Become dim
And the universe
Stands lifeless

Transform

Waking from a slumber

The rise and fall of your chest

Taking in the breath of a new day

As you emerge

Ready to transform

To make your way

From one skin

To another

Stars

It's all in the stars

The secrets of yesterday

The surprises of tomorrow

If only they could speak

And If only we would listen

Possibility

Maybe words will flow

Endlessly and free

Inspired by the sea

Something new to say

Somewhere new to be

Time to breathe

A fresh wave

Of possibilities

Short of Breath

I feel like I'm gasping for air

Grasping for substance

And I'm left empty handed

And short of breath

Could You Feel

Imagine what the world would be like

Through the eyes of someone blind

Imagine what the world would sound like

Through the ears of someone deaf

Could you feel the shadows

Could you feel the silence

Secrets

The snow drifts

The imagination blows

The beauty surrenders

And everybody knows

Irony

Irony dances

With the stars

Time flies

With the shadows of the night

You remain out of sight

Quicksand

Don't look back

Don't get lost in the sea

Of memories

Treasure them

Take them

Take all that you are

Don't stumble

Don't fall

Don't get stuck

In the quicksand of regret

Realm

I fall asleep in

 one realm of beauty

And awake

 in another

Deafening

The desert sands

Scream

The intensity

Of the heat is deafening

Alive

The breath of night

The voice of light

Reveal the path

The enlightened path

That in one moment

And in many moments

You choose to follow

And with each step

You become more alive

Subsides

The raging tempest subsides

Revealing innocence and beauty

With the sweet scent of spring

Here

There is a place

That if I allow myself to enter

When I leave

I am filled

With this enormous inspiration

And a sense of rebirth

The Search

In this strange and twisted world

We come across broken hearts

Lost souls and dying love

Every person

Searching for their smile

Some have already found it

And some never will

When and if

we find what we are looking for

We also find the fear of losing it

Whisper

Sometimes I think

I heard the secret

Whispered by the breath of life

And sometimes I think

I just misunderstood

Dissolve

Are you watching me dissolve

As I sink into the sand

Melt into the earth

I was seeking higher ground

But this is what I found

Time stands still

And I'm surrounded by the thick

Sound of silence

I can feel the world spin

As my spirit is released

Into the stars

Free

Free

But also lost

Happy

but at what cost

Searching

Flying

Hoping to land

Feet in the sand

Beauty

Such a vast amount of beauty

In this life

In this day

In this night

Hidden in every corner

Of every soul

And every spirit

Created for one purpose or another

The Race

Your heart races by
You try to catch up
But your breath
Is held hostage
By your lungs
Trapped by your anxiety
You power through
Knocking fear
To its knees
The breath of life escapes
Air blows free
You hear the rhythm of your pulse
Dancing in your ears
Your vision clears
It's time to take that step
Onto the path
Take that leap
into the journey
Listen to the rhythm of your pulse
As your feet follow
In the footsteps of your heart

Chapters

As you read

Through the chapters

Of your life

Do you recognize

The twisted words

Of a tortured soul

A forgotten voice

Can you see your reflection

In the darkness

Don't get sucked in

Don't let them swallow you

Turn on the light

New love

New life

A blank page

Awaits

Look

Look into the night

Look into the sea

Search for the soul

You want to be

Search for the place

Where you belong

Listen to the song

See the truth in the

Reflections of the moon

It shines upon you

Like the brightest star

It shows you who you are

As you sink into the sand

You begin to understand

Unravelling

Bursting at the seams

Letting it all go

As it flows from my soul

My past, my present

My thoughts, emotions

All onto the page

Line after line

Time after time

 left wide open

Revealed , exposed

Raw and vulnerable

Unraveled

Inhale

Inhale

Take it all in

Sight

Smell

Taste

Sound

Hold it all in

A memory created

Exhale

Let it all go

Let it fall

Onto the page

Eyes Open Wide

Alive with wonder

Time to dive in

Where the story begins

Where the water meets the sky

Eyes open wide

Alive with wonder

Time to dive in

Where will the story end

Where the water meets the sky

A Forgotten Sound

There you are again

Swimming around in my head

Where have you been

Why did you fade away

Was there nothing more to say

Did the colors of my passion dim

From the vivid to the grey

Or were you always there,

A forgotten sound

Hidden in the corners of my mind

Just watching the time go by

Waiting to be found

Waiting for your expression

Pride

Watching you fly

through the air

With grace and power

I so admire

You land perfectly

Your smile is free

And I'm overcome with pride

Disguise

You never asked
And I never said
That doesn't make it any less true
I hate that it hurts you
I hope you understand
It's in my head
It's out of my hands
It might seem random
Out of the blue
It's always been there
I never wore a mask
Never a disguise
I'm surprised by your surprise
I thought you knew me better
I thought you read my letter
I thought you could
see it in my eyes

The Sun of Summer

I'm dreaming of

The sun of summer

The sky above

The warmth of love

The sound of the surf

The sun of summer

Waves rolling in

Touching my skin

With the spray of salt

 Bringing my breath

To a halt

The sun of summer

I'm dreaming of

Drive

On a drive

Open sky

Hair blows

In the wind

Music streams

Loud and free

Sun on your face

Taste of air

On a drive

To somewhere

To everywhere

To nowhere

And back again

Poetry

The words are there

Poetry

Restlessly waiting

To be set free

To paint the picture

Tell the story

Of the life

Of you and me

The love the laughter

The before and after

Grief

It was so hard to see you

The loss, the misery

A sea of memories

A hollow vacancy

I reached for you

But I fell in too

The loss, the misery

A sea of memories

A hollow vacancy

So I guess we will

Ride the waves of grief

Together in disbelief

Until the tide subsides

Born

I wanted and I waited

Impatiently patient

Finally you were born

Into our lives

Warming up the bones of winter

Created by our love

Created for our love

Creating so much love

I hope I show you

As I hold you in my arms

I'll never let you go

I hope you know

I'll always be here

To watch you grow

Alivia

Our love created

A beautiful soul

A being full of love

With her true colors

Radiant and bright

A rainbow of light

That shines through her skin

A spirit

Free and full of life

Brave and strong

One that faces her fears

Rights her wrongs

She is a dream realized

A wish granted

A gift to treasure

As we unwrap her love

Every day as she grows

Just like our love

That created

A beautiful soul

Unwrap the Surprises

When the sun sets and rises

When the moon is new and full

When the stars shine bright

In the blackest night

Maybe it's time

To climb the mountain

Maybe it's time

To sail the sea

Embrace the mystery

Unwrap the surprises

Let It Be Free

Don't analyze the art

It doesn't need a label

It doesn't need validation

Take in the beauty

Unique expression

Let it touch your heart

Create inspiration

Let it be free

Let it Move Me

I'm so sorry

I forgot to listen

Can you play the song again

I promise to pay attention

To find the meaning in the lyrics

Feel the rhythm

Beneath the surface

Let it move me

Gaze

Maybe if you step aside

Get out of your own way

Shift your gaze

You will see your reflection

Find the power of perception

Home

How can I ever leave you

When I do

Will you remain the same

An empty box

Full of memories

For me to come back to

Magic

Tank is empty

Low on fuel

Wait.

When the time is right

Inspiration will strike

Ignite the spark

Spread like wildfire

Fill up on the magic

Let it drive you

Are You Ready?

Is it time yet

For the Sun to rise

To meet the sky

To bring the light

And are you ready

For the flight

Shadows

The shadows are looming

And I can only assume

That this night is endless

The trees are monstrous

The hours, timeless

And I'm lost

In the magic of the stars

That are falling

At the speed of light

Slowly fading

Out of sight

Reoccurring Dream

I'm climbing the trees
And the branches are broken
I've listened to the secrets
The breeze has spoken
I whispered them to you
In a reoccurring dream
Where nothing is what it seems
And the treacherous depths
Of reality seem to gleam
In the brilliance of this night
Full of screams
I've lost my sight
Trying to fight
The blinding light
Forever goodnight

Twinkling

Stars are falling from the sky

I see them twinkling in your eyes

I put them there to light your way

The day that I died

Stuck

I'm standing still
I'm trying to fly
I'm stuck in the shadows
I'm trying to follow
I'm crying but my eyes are dry
I'm trying to swallow
I choke on my words
I can see my escape
I'm alive but hollow
I'm trying to fly
But I will
Survive

Echo

I hear your voice

Echoing in my soul

And I can't make sense

Of the words

They seem to be out of your control

Because they are empty

And I recognize

Their transparency

Broken Down

Sometimes I feel so broken down

Like I'm going nowhere

With nothing stopping me

Just sitting by the side of the road

Waiting for something

Wilting

My spirit is wilting

Fading into the darkness

Of the night

My energy is being pulled

From the heavens

And from the earth

My soul is caught in the middle of the war

Which is quickly

Leading to my destruction

The extinguishing of my fire

No Absolution

There is no absolution

In this world

There is a little light

In every shadow

And a little darkness

In every light

Pieces

Didn't you see me fall apart

Didn't you see my shattered heart

Don't you remember

You picked up the pieces

Tired

I'm tired of being awake

And I'm tired of being asleep

And I wish there was somewhere

 I could go in between

Key

It's as if I'm locked inside my soul

With an infinite amount of words

Dying to escape

Dying to reveal

My identity

And all I can do is write

And hope that someone hears my voice

Someone finds the key

Stay Afloat

Lost and searching

Through blurred vision

For some reality

In this sea of eternal dreams

Trying to stay afloat

The waves of time

Which wash over you

Each one with an attempt

To take away the

Breath of life

A Realm of Contentment

My hell is a sleep with no dreams

With a solitary awakening

In a world full of screams

And Isolation

A Black Sea drowns the lost souls

That only wanted to be free

My heaven is an enlightenment

A great inspiration

A world where dreams and reality

Go hand in hand

And everyone understands

the beauty in simplicity

And the spirits of the lost souls

Are free to wander aimlessly

In a realm of contentment

Heal

When the passion

That once burned like fire

Turns to ice

When your spirit

That was once so free

Is confined within itself

When your skin

Has lost its sense of touch

And your lips forgot how to really feel

When your tears are frozen

And your mind is blown

And your heart

Can no longer trust

The only way to heal

Is to find what's real

Thorns

I'm lying here

In this bed of roses

My skin is numb to the thorns

That scorn my soul

I've never been this close

Tears are melting my spirit

I'm no longer whole

As I burn and bleed

Becoming just a shadow of creation

An image of temptation

Controlled by the sensation

Of this time and space

And nobody knows

The pain of the rose

Deep

You are never quite

Out of my mind

Deep in the waters

Of my soul

Deep in the rivers

Of my blood

So deeply

In touch

Tick of the Clock

All the time in the world

To go nowhere

All the space in the world

To create this void

I can't tolerate the silence

I can't break the ice it creates

I can feel my world shatter

And my heart stop

With the tick of the clock

I wonder if everything

that has been created

Ceased to exist

If the world would just

Exist in peace

Or if any world would exist at all

Fear

Fear is the shadow

That feeds hesitation

It's the seed that stems

Jealousy anger loneliness

It grows into bitter paranoia

And does nothing but damage

Hunger

A hunger so great

It cannot be satisfied

A thirst so great

It cannot be quenched

An ache so deep

It cannot be touched

And a desire

So vast

So real

It can only be filled

By your taste

Your touch

Your love

In My Mind

Your absence

 is the alarm

That awakens

The hunger

The craving

For your presence

Your taste

Your touch

Your smell

I close my eyes

And blindly

Paint the picture of you

 in my mind

Breathless

Trembling

Overwhelmed by the ecstasy

Your taste

Your touch

Creates

And the peace that fills my soul

Like the sweet breath of sleep

Touch

Touch can heal so much

And with each touch

Your soul burns brighter

Always

Your face is one I will always see

Your voice is one

I will always hear

Your presence is one

I will always feel

Your love I will always cherish

Your soul is one

Mine will never forget

Passing Seconds

I'm suddenly very much aware

Of the time

Of each passing second,

 as the time without you

Creeps along

The aching loneliness

Inside of me is growing rapidly

Captured

Like the fire

 dancing in the moonlight

Catches your eye

You've captured my soul

And I can't look away

Because I am amazed

By your beauty

And the fire it contains

Full

I'm so full of love for you

It empowers me

Inspires me

Lifts my spirit

When I have fallen

Anchored

You have swept me off my feet

Like an unexpected wave

You have brought me a gift

Of infinite pleasure

A treasure so vast, so great

I can't help but be anchored

By your love

Distance

When we are apart

A longing fills my heart

My soul is incomplete

My body is cold

My smile fades

When I see your face

My smile returns

My soul is whole

Joy fills my heart

A spark ignites

Butterflies release

My body shivers and burns

At your touch

I still feel so much

In love

Balance

Find the balance

When the stars align

Feel the words tip toe

Across the high wires of your heart

Don't let them fall

Into the ravine of the never mind

Don't let them be blown away

By the winds of your soul

Become dust in the sands of time

Energy

Can you feel the energy

Crackle and fizz

An electric current

Beneath the skin

Absorb the ecstasy

Let it fill you to the brink

Spill into your life

Take A Moment

It's okay to take a moment

To let your soul shine

It's okay to choose the path

That lights you up inside

It's okay to love the path

 you choose to follow

And the one that Lead you to it

All Consuming

The mountains consume the air

Flowers dance in their shadows

Blooms in shades of sunshine

Tickled by the breeze

Raindrops begin to fall

Quench their thirst

Inhale the scent

Drink in the beauty

All consuming

Tremble of the Universe

Can you feel the quake

Of the earth

Can you feel the shift

Of the stars

Can you feel the stillness

A profound moment

The pause of time

At the edge of change

Subtle yet defining

Can you feel the quake

Of the earth

The tremble of

The universe

Open

Open the windows

To your mind

Open the doors

To your soul

Let the stale

Stagnant air escape

The negativity go

Inhale the fresh air

Welcome creativity

And inspiration

Awaken the senses

Revive the spirit

Unwind the mind

Feel more

Alive

Sunset

Wrapped in the arms

Of the sunset

Gaze upon the horizon

Water reflects the colors

Painted by the sky

Listen to the tides speak

Of wild surprises

As they crash

upon the shore

Wrapped in the arms

Of peace

Gaze upon the horizon

Revel in the beauty

As it reveals what's more

Swallowed

A stone

Cast into

The river of life

Skims across the surface

Ripples spread like wrinkles

A stone

Swept up by the current

Swallowed by the

Brittle bones of time

About the Author

I have been writing since I was 17. It has always been an outlet for me to express myself. To me, poetry is painting with words. I love creating a vivid picture in the mind of the reader. I have an amazing husband and beautiful daughter that inspire me every day.

My passions include family, sunshine, yoga, poetry, painting, and the ocean. It is my hope that my words will inspire others in some small way, as many writers have inspired me.

Made in the USA
Monee, IL
06 December 2019